The Behavioural Sciences

techniques of application

Patrick A Sills

University of York

Institute of Personnel Management
5 Winsley Street, Oxford Circus, London W1N 7AQ

First published 1973

ISBN 0 85292 088 1

Set in 11 pt Garamond

This publication was originally prepared in response to a request from Shell International Petroleum Co Ltd and with the encouragement of Philip Sadler, Principal of Ashridge Management College. I would like to acknowledge, and thank them for their part in this wider publication of the material.

Printed in Great Britain
by Cox & Wyman Ltd, London, Reading and Fakenham

Contents

Introduction

Chapter

Diagnostic Techniques

1	Records analysis and manpower forecasting	7
2	Human asset accounting	9
3	Tests and the early identification of management potential	10
4	The interview	13
5	Attitude and opinion surveys	14
6	Behavioural analysis	15
7	Ergonomics	16
8	Socio-technical systems analysis	17

Training Techniques

1	T-groups	19
2	The managerial grid (Blake)	20
3	Practice of management principles (Coverdale)	21
4	Problem analysis and decision making (Kepner and Tregoe)	22
5	The 3-D organizational effectiveness programme (Reddin)	24
6	Training for leadership (Adair)	28
7	Achievement – motivation (McLelland)	29
8	The technology of training	31

Change – facilitation techniques

1	Job enrichment	34
2	Planned change	35
3	Participative management	36
4	Management by objectives	39
5	Action research	40
6	Organizational development learning	41
	Conclusion	42

Introduction

This short publication is intended to provide a synopsis of the main 'developments' in the research-and-development continuum of the behavioural sciences. It is the intention to describe each technique in summary form only, but recommendations on further references to particular topics are supplied. The discussion will be descriptive and will not attempt comparison or evaluation except in general terms.

The techniques available can be broadly classified into three categories: tools for *diagnosing* problem areas; *training* methods and programmes; and the third has been designed to *facilitate organizational change and development*. The individual techniques will be discussed under these three headings.

DIAGNOSTIC TECHNIQUES

1 Records analysis and manpower forecasting

Many organizations produce statistics on labour turnover, absenteeism, accident rates etc; but their significance is often unnoticed because the analytical breakdowns are not in meaningful and managerially controllable categories (eg management can do little about an overall labour turnover of 10 per cent but a lot about Section Y's turnover of 30 per cent).

Relatively few organizations collect and produce statistics on employee age, educational qualifications, career potential etc; yet these frequently reveal significant comparative differences when interrelated with labour turnover, for example; in addition, the information is essential to manpower control and forecasting.

Manpower forecasting is a developing technique which applies sophisticated statistical measurements to record analysis in two main problem areas:

1 *Projection of future manpower needs*, both completely and in relevant categories and organizational departments.

This is derived from analysis of historical manpower trends in relation to concurrent trends in other aspects of organizational performance (for instance in the oil industry refinery throughput, material load, truckage etc). To the extent that

past trends are likely to continue

consistent relationships are discovered between manpower structure and performance indices and

target performance trends have been predetermined,

future manpower requirements can be accurately predicted.

The following model illustrates the manpower demand forecasting process.

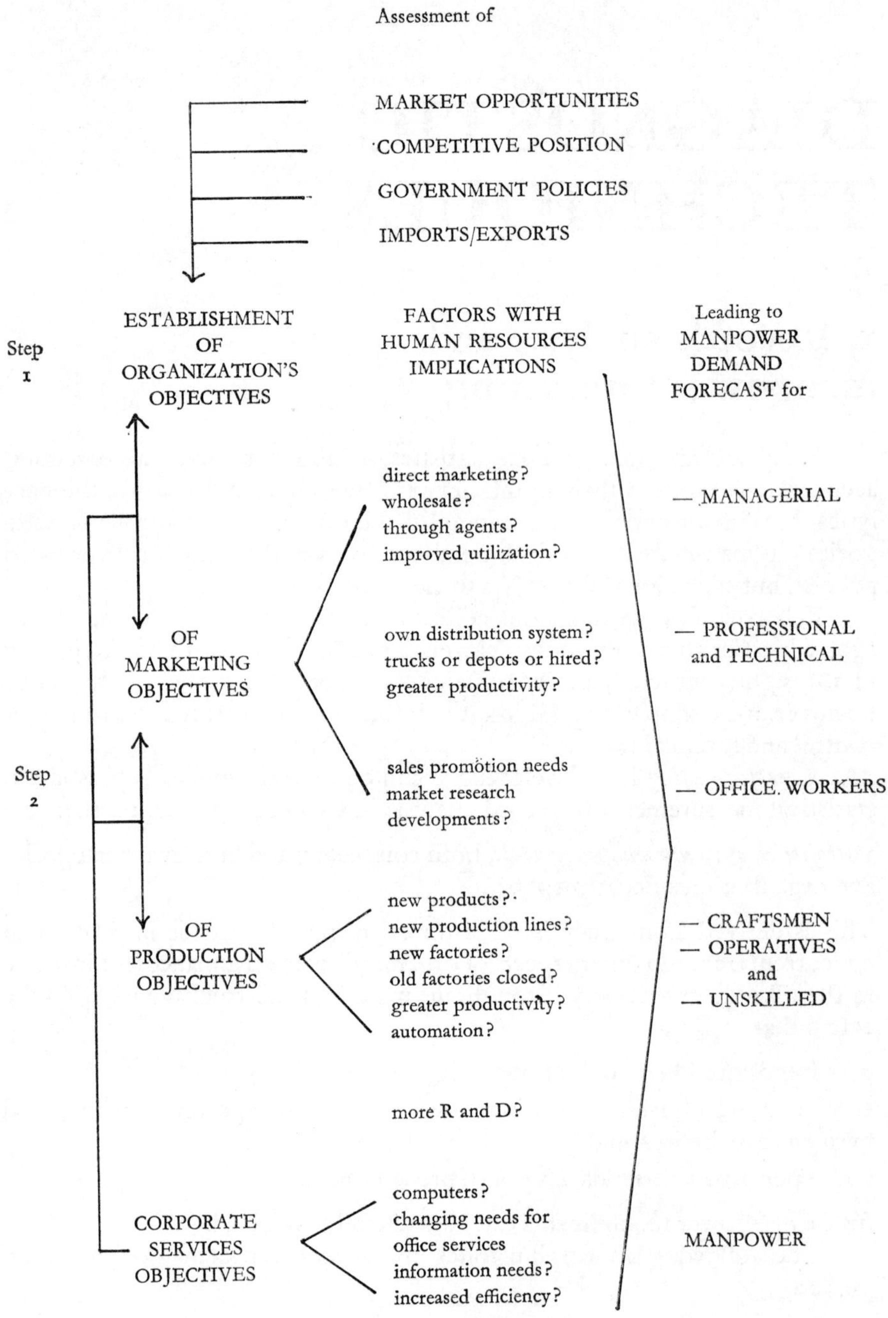
Assessment of
MARKET OPPORTUNITIES
COMPETITIVE POSITION
GOVERNMENT POLICIES
IMPORTS/EXPORTS
Step 1
ESTABLISHMENT OF ORGANIZATION'S OBJECTIVES
FACTORS WITH HUMAN RESOURCES IMPLICATIONS
Leading to MANPOWER DEMAND FORECAST for
direct marketing?
wholesale?
through agents?
improved utilization?
— MANAGERIAL
OF MARKETING OBJECTIVES
own distribution system?
trucks or depots or hired?
greater productivity?
— PROFESSIONAL and TECHNICAL
Step 2
sales promotion needs
market research
developments?
— OFFICE WORKERS
OF PRODUCTION OBJECTIVES
new products?
new production lines?
new factories?
old factories closed?
greater productivity?
automation?
— CRAFTSMEN
— OPERATIVES
and
— UNSKILLED
more R and D?
CORPORATE SERVICES OBJECTIVES
computers?
changing needs for
office services
information needs?
increased efficiency?
MANPOWER

2 *Manpower utilization*: One achievement of manpower forecasters has been to develop a broad application of the manpower/workload ratio originally employed in work study. Comparative indices have been established for assessing manpower productivity, but further developments will be dependent on improved analysis of job content and objectives and the consequential setting of future manpower targets.

References

Perspectives in Manpower Planning, Edinburgh Group, IPM, 1967
Manpower Planning, Gareth Stainer, Heinemann, 1971

2 Human asset accounting

The need is increasingly being realized not only for this improvement of manpower planning but also the measurement of manpower resources in financial terms. Likert argues that the following attributes of an organization could be expressed in monetary valuations:

"Level of intelligence and aptitudes
Level of training
Level of performance goals and motivation to achieve organizational success
Quality of leadership
Capacity to use differences for purposes of innovation and improvement, rather than allowing differences to develop into bitter, irreconcilable, interpersonal conflict
Quality of communication upward, downward and laterally
Quality of decision making
Capacity to achieve cooperative teamwork versus competitive striving for personal success at the expense of the organization
Quality of the control processes of the organization and the levels of felt responsibility which exist
Capacity to achieve effective coordination
Capacity to use experience and measurements to guide decisions, improve operations and introduce innovations."

Two main approaches are being developed:

Start-up costs, ie the cost of hiring and training personnel and developing them 'into a coordinated organization operating in a reasonably satisfactory manner'.

Replacement costs of the overall human resources of an organization plus the 'synergistic component', ie the firm's investment in establishing effective cooperative working relationships. Estimates of the replacement costs of more and less productive organizations vary between 10x and 2x current payroll.

Although this work is embryonic, the redress of the historical imbalance in investment appraisal should induce organizations to consider their human resources less as cost centres and more as asset centres which require maintenance and development.

References

The Human Organization (Chapter 9) R Likert, McGraw-Hill, 1967
see also *Human Asset Accounting*, J Giles and D F Robinson, IPM, 1972

3 Tests and the early identification of management potential

Aptitude and personality tests developed by behavioural scientists are already extensively used in industry. Aptitude tests measure, for example vision, hearing, simple motor skills, spatial aptitude, mechanical comprehension, clerical and computational aptitudes. Personality tests are less frequently used but are particularly applicable to jobs requiring considerable interpersonal contact. The tests most widely used in selection are interest tests, personality inventories, projective techniques and situational tests.

Interest tests record individuals' like and dislike of activities, objects or types of people commonly encountered in daily living; these are sometimes classified into:

Occupational interest areas – mechanical, scientific, persuasive and artistic.
Value constructs, eg theoretical, economic, aesthetic, social, political and religious.
Approaches to interpersonal relationships – the relative importance to an individual of support, conformity, recognition, independence, benevolence and leadership.

Personality inventories are a battery of test items designed to produce comparative scores on different personality traits. The Guilford-Zimmerman Temperament Survey scores ten traits: general activity, restraint, ascendancy, sociability, emotional stability, objectivity, friendliness, thoughtfulness, personal relations and masculinity. Cattell's 16 Personality Factor Test Profile measures extroversion/introversion, intelligence, emotional stability, aggressiveness, carefreeness, conscientiousness, interpersonal spontaneity, tender-mindedness/toughmindedness, trust, conventionality, shrewdness, guilt proneness, radicalism, self-sufficiency, self-discipline, anxiety proneness.
Projective techniques provide the subject with a vague and/or uncompleted stimulus and assess his reactions and interpretations. The Thematic Apperception Test consists of a series of pictures on which subjects are requested to base a story. The Rorschach Ink-blot Test presents an ink-blot which subjects are asked to identify and describe. Story and sentence completion tests also initiate generalized personality response with deliberately unstructured introductions.
Situational tests are designed to measure emotional, social, attitudinal and other personality traits reflected by behaviour in simulated conditions. Two industrially applicable examples are 'country-house' selection techniques and leaderless group discussions.

One particularly imaginative and pioneering use of test results is the '*Early Identification of Management Potential*' research programme carried out in Exxon Corporation (formerly Standard Oil Company of New Jersey). This aimed to establish factors on which a successful career in the company could be predicted, and based its conclusions on analysis of the test results of 443 managers at different levels in the organization. Although other tests were completed by these managers, the seven which discriminated between the more and less successful managers, to a statistically significant degree, were:

Miller Analogies Test (a high level verbal test assessing general mental ability)
Analytical Reasoning Test (non-verbal)
Guilford-Zimmerman Temperament Survey (self-description of attitudes, views and feelings)
Personal History Inventory (early years)
Personal History Inventory (later years)
Performance Report (self-description of performance on the job)
Management Judgement Test (assessing orientation toward different business situations).

The criteria used as evidence of management success were:

Position-level achieved in the organization
Salory-progression
Managerial effectiveness as appraised by immediate managers

A single measure of success was obtained through factor analysis, this measure being weighted to eliminate the effect of age, and length of service, differences. This was designated the success criterion. Similarly, managers' test results were cumulated into a weighted score. When the weighted test scores were correlated with the success criterion indices, it was shown that managers with a test score in the top 20 per cent were about nineteen times more likely to be in the top success group than those whose scores were in the bottom 20 per cent.

The chances in 100 of being in the most successful third of managers were:

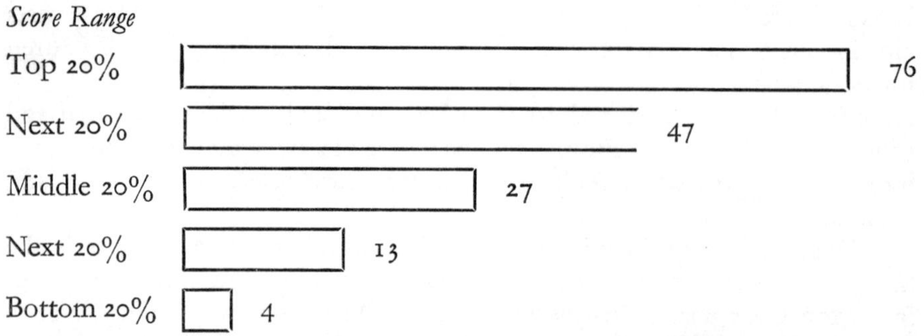

The tests which correlated most highly with managerial success were the personal history inventories. This 'is a sort of personality test which measures such characteristics as independence, maturity, sociability, social responsibility, and certain kinds of vocational and avocational interests'. The test results which had the second highest correlation with the success criterion were obtained from the Management Judgement Test.

In those Exxon organizations which are using the tests, professional and supervisory employees complete part of the battery soon after joining the company (those tests which measure characteristics which are extrinsic to an individual's work experience, for example the Miller Analogies Test and the Personal History Inventory, early years). The tests measuring managerial judgement, self-performance appraisal and later personal history are administered after about five years of service.

Uncover promising employees at an early stage in their career
Assist promotional choice
Encourage early action on unpromising men
Provide a yardstick for evaluating the achievement of recruitment objectives
Develop more accurate appraisal techniques.

The results have been validated over 15 years and in Exxon operations in USA, Canada, and several other countries (including some in Europe). The test battery may not be directly transferable from Exxon Corporation to other companies; but appropriate batteries with similarly significant correlations between test scores and managerial success are likely to be of importance to other companies' operations in the future.

Reference

Summary Report of the Early Identification of Management Potential Research Project, Social Science Research Division, Standard Oil Company, 1961

4 The interview

The interview is a behavioural science tool which is used extensively for selection and appraisal in organizations. The 'dos' and 'don'ts' of interviewing are outlined in several books (eg *The Skills of Interviewing*, by E Sidney and M Brown, Tavistock, 1961) but the *results* of interviewing have been subject to relatively little investigation.

Two recent studies throw light on the dynamics of appraisal interviewing.

From an analysis of 1440 appraisal forms from six companies, interviews with 20 managers and questionnaire replies from 40 managers undergoing training, K H Rowe concluded that (i) appraisers were reluctant to appraise; this was reflected both in the high proportion of uncompleted forms and in the tendency of managers to select the middle and immediately higher box in the five fold forced choice (in all the firms except one, no less than 84 per cent of those appraised were 'satisfactory' or more than adequate); (ii) interviewers are even more reluctant to interview; interviews are frequently either not held or very brief; (iii) follow-up is inadequate; no relation was discovered between action to transfer managers or send them on training courses and recommendations to this effect on appraisal forms.

The recommendations arising from this study included:

The importance of appraisal must be emphasized to all managers
Appraisals should be based on present performance
The best person to conduct appraisal is the appraisee's immediate boss;

Subordinates should participate more in the appraisal process
Recommendations must be clearly stated and adequately followed up.

H H Meyer conducted an experiment in a large GEC plant in USA in which 92 employees were involved. Half these employees were appraised with high participation techniques and half with low participation techniques. The employees were interviewed and completed questionnaires before and after their appraisal and each appraisal interview was recorded and observed by research staff. The conclusions from this study included:

Criticism has negative effects on performance and subordinate evaluation of performance
Performance improves most when specific goals are established
The improvement of performance should be a continuing and not a once-a-year activity
Interviews concerned with improving performance should not be concerned at the same time with salary reviews or promotion prospects

Subordinate participation in the setting of performance targets increases both commitment to, and success in, achieving them. The authors recommend a 'work planning and review' approach to appraisal.

References

An Appraisal of Appraisals, K H Rowe, *Journal of Management Studies*, Vol I, No 1, 1964
Split Roles in Performance Appraisal, H H Meyer *et al*, *Harvard Business Review*, Jan/Feb, 1965
Staff Appraisal, G A Randell *et al*, IPM, 1972

5 Attitude and opinion surveys

Opinion surveys are usually conducted through the medium of a questionnaire designed to elicit respondents' views on particular issues. Questionnaire completion is optional and anonymous by either the whole or a representative sample of the 'population' concerned. Issues on which employees' opinions have been explored through the use of this technique include remuneration, working conditions, fringe benefits, unionization, training policies etc.

The technique is particularly valuable when a change is envisaged which will affect large groups of employees. It provides a quick method for identifying likely employee reactions to planned changes.

The questionnaires used in *attitude surveys* attempt to delve into more permanent and fundamental feelings of respondents rather than (though often in addition to) their opinions on specific topics. Questions are asked about attitudes to the company, management and job content which can be of longer-term use to management than a special opinion poll. The distinguishing administrative feature of attitude surveys is a series of unstructured interviews with approximately 10 per cent of the eventual sample which are conducted before the questionnaire is designed and distributed. This enables the investigators to explore in depth the main issues on which attitudes are strongly held in order to ensure the most appropriate questionnaire design.

Attitudes and opinions are usually explored in the same survey. Some companies are already committed to inviting their employees to participate in surveys not only once but at regular (eg two-yearly) intervals. This enables them to build up a bank of data from which comparisons can be drawn, not only between different parts of the company at the same time but also the same parts at different times. Some companies feel that the importance of monitoring and accounting employee attitudes and opinions is as great as utilizing control information about more tangible employee characteristics.

Reference

Measuring Morale and Motivation. T G P Rogers, *Management Decision* Winter 1968

6 Behavioural analysis

Job analysis, task analysis and skills analysis are separate techniques available for breaking down requisite behaviour in a job into its constituent parts. Two methods for analysing *actual* work behaviour are diary-keeping and activity sampling. Overall job content is broken down into meaningful categories and the time spent on each recorded by oneself or an observer. The five categories used by Carlson in a recent study of company directors in Sweden were:

Location
Time spent with other people and who they were
Methods of communication
The nature of the questions handled (eg which function, whether they were short-or long-term and whether they concerned policy or application)
The kind of action (eg getting information, taking decisions, giving orders, inspecting and reviewing).

These categories can be recorded continuously or in time-blocks, as is usually done with diary-keeping, or at regular intervals, as with activity sampling.

Diary-keeping is particularly revealing in providing interpretation as well as description of events, but it places an increased strain on managers and tends to rely on their memory (for the weakness of which the technique is attempting to compensate).

Activity sampling is the most objective method of recording behaviour. It involves the recording at regular intervals of the particular activities in which subjects are engaged; and it provides an accurate pattern of overall behaviour if the statistical rules of representative selection of behavioural items are adhered to. The method can be relieved of its comparative clinicism by the simultaneous recording of event-sequences (particular activities can then be seen in the context of their relatively long-term objectives) and case studies of incidents which illustrate microcosmically but intensively some of the problems under investigation.

The results of both analytical methods are highly revealing to managers and it is likely that their industrial application will become increasingly popular.

Reference

Managers and their jobs, R Stewart, Macmillan, 1967

7 Ergonomics

Ergonomics (sometimes known as engineering psychology) is principally concerned with the interaction of man and machine as constituent elements of a total man/machine system. Ergonomists point out that the average lathe in this country is designed for a man $4\frac{1}{2}'$ tall, $2'$ across the shoulders with an $8'$ arm span and stress the importance of analysing man and machine as a total working unit.

In the design of machines ergonomists pay particular attention to the effects on the operator and his decisions, of displays (the sensory input to the operation), controls (the motor output from the operator), panel layout and display-control compatibility.

In the man-machine's immediate 'workspace' ergonomists analyse the influence on the man's position, posture and reach of machine size and structure, chairs, desks etc and adjacent machines, structures and materials.

In the man-machine's wider environment ergonomists analyse the influence on man's behaviour and performance of physical factors (eg light and colour, noise, heat, ventilation, gravity, movement, electromagnetic and nuclear radiation), chemical factors (eg gas or liquid, composition, pressure, smell), biological factors (eg microbes, insects, animals) and psychological factors (eg discomfort or risk, intelligence, skill, suitability for the job, training needs).

References

Ergonomics for Industry, Department of Scientific and Industrial Research Series of Pamphlets,
Journal of Applied Ergonomics

8 Socio-technical system analysis

The word 'system' has two main connotations: a system is a total entity made up of interdependent constituent parts; a system is also one part of a wider whole, with which it is in a state of interaction; a system therefore imports energy or raw material from its environment, transforms this through the interrelated operation of its parts and exports its 'product' back to its environment. The 'socio-technical' systems approach has been developed by the Tavistock Institute of Human Relations; while it incorporates both definitions of 'system' it concentrates on two constituent parts which are both critical and highly interdependent.

The technical sub-system consists of the materials, machines, techniques and processes which form the technology of the organization. The social sub-system comprises a series of work-roles and the network of relationships which connect these work-roles together. It defines for each individual the behaviour expected from him in order that the organization might achieve its objectives; it also defines the expected behaviour of other employees with whom an individual is likely to interact in the overall working of the organization. The technical and social sub-systems are closely related in the sense that a change in one is likely to lead to changes in the other.

This approach has not yet been refined sufficiently to enable a checklist of critical items to be compiled. Miller and Rice of the Tavistock Institute have concluded, however, that the following conditions are critical to work groups both in the achievement of their tasks and in meeting the human needs of their members:

1 A task must be such that those engaged on its parts can experience, as a group, completion of the whole task

2 A group must be able to regulate its own activities and be judged by its results
3 A group must be of such a size that it can not only regulate its own activities but also provide satisfactory personal relationships
4 The range of skills required in a group for task performance should not be so great as to reinforce external affiliations and thus induce internal differentiations; nor should status differences within the group be large enough to inhibit internal mobility
5 A group should not be unique, so that those who have become disaffected have no alternative group engaged in a similar task and requiring similar skills and experience to which they can move. Otherwise an individual's investment in one group is likely to be so great as to distort his values and judgements, and the possibility of his expulsion so threatening as to be destructive.
6 Task/technical change must be accompanied by the following considerations which should be taken into account in the planning of work groups:
   (a) members of groups should share a common belief in the objectives of their secondary group (department or organization); the indispensability of the secondary group will increasingly be dependent on its constituent parts
   (b) 'to maintain adaptiveness, greatest sentience (ie emotional commitment) must remain invested in groups committed to change'
   (c) the preservation of adequate emotional commitment to the group will often depend on finding or inventing other groups on whom can be projected feelings and behaviour that, if retained within the group, would destroy its own cohesion.

Reference

Systems of Organization, E J Miller and A K Rice, Tavistock, 1967. *Reproduced by permission.*

TRAINING TECHNIQUES

1 T-groups

T-groups (an abbreviation for training groups) aim to 'increase a person's sensitivity to and knowledge about personal and interpersonal factors and their influences on thought and action and to help him in his efforts to behave more effectively in different and changing interpersonal relationships'. It is 'an approach to human relations training which is aimed at getting people to *feel* and *behave* differently and not merely to *think* differently with reference to the day to day handling of human problems'.

The common denominators of all T-group training are:

The absence of group task and group structure
Concentration on the processes of interpersonal behaviour in the group. This is the group's only subject matter. Its only task is to make sense of this experience
The trainer is not only non-judgemental but also non-directive. His role is to interpret the group to itself.

The issues which usually promote most discussion are authority, power and leadership, group structure and procedure and the interpersonal dynamics of individual member relationships.

Variations on the T-group theme are:

Laboratory learning – the development of interpersonal skills through practice and feedback but not necessarily through involvement in continuous group activity
Process groups. These groups are formed to achieve a specific task but are additionally committed to the sub-task of monitoring their own interpersonal behaviour
Laboratory groups. These are natural work groups which meet together outside their everyday situations to discuss improvements in working effectiveness. In addition to their concern with common work problems and goals, they often discuss intra-group communication and interpersonal relationships.

Reference

T-group Training: Group Dynamics in Management Education, G Whitaker. Association of Teachers in Management, Occasional Paper 2, 1965

2 The managerial grid

Grid Organization Development is based on a model of managerial commitment evolved by R R Blake and J S Mouton. They postulate that a manager's two main concerns, production and people, can be matrixed on a graph and that managers are likely to fall in one of five positions:

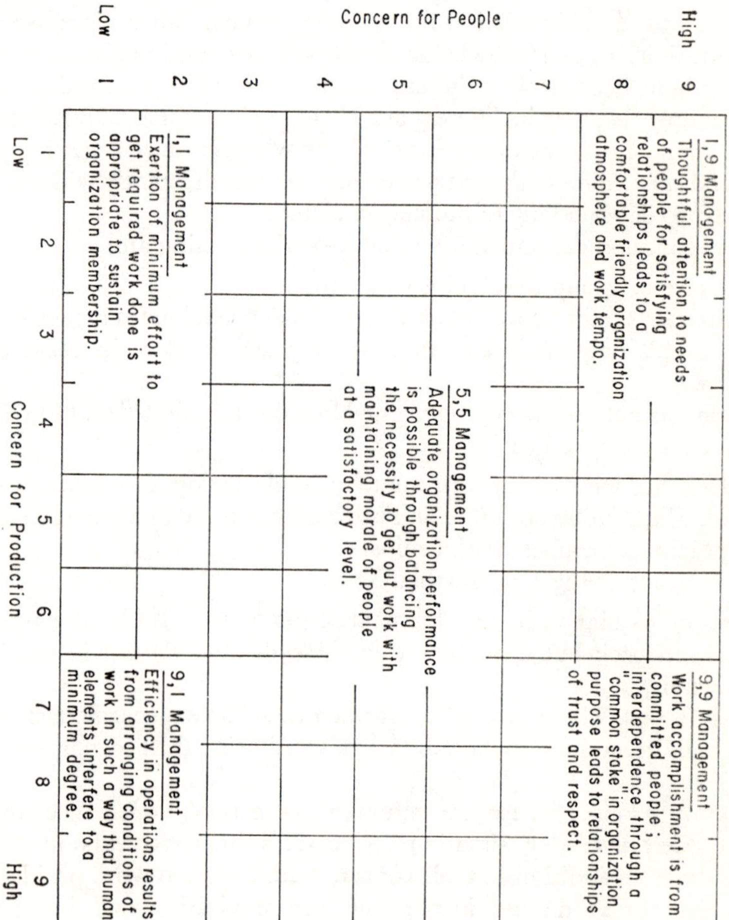

The object of the training programme based on this model is to develop 9·9 managers and to 'achieve production through mature interpersonal relationships which are integrated with the purposes of the organization'. Training is broken up into six discrete phases during which participants take account of production requirements, people requirements and the third 'organizational universal', the hierarchy.

The first part of the programme is called 'Management Development within an Organization' and consists of two phases. Phase I is aimed at making participants familiar with the assumptions and terms of the Managerial Grid and contains structured experiments to show how interpersonal relationships affect task accomplishments. Participants also receive face-to-face feedback about their personal managerial styles. Phase II is attended by natural work groups which explore their individual managerial styles in greater depth and examine their operating practices as a work team.

The second part of the training programme, Organizational Development, consists of four phases. Phase III is designed to improve horizontal and vertical intergroup problem solving by involving two teams in establishing the image of their own and the other group; the phase culminates in the two teams discussing their conclusions. Phase IV involves two exercises in 'setting organizational improvement goals'; the first is carried out by a diagonal slice' group (the group members come from different parts of the organization) and the second by work teams. Phase V consists of implementing the planned change by attaining the group's established goals. This is carried over into the work place and a specialist monitors improvement. Phase VI consists of 'stabilization' of the organizational improvements.

References

The Managerial Grid, R R Blake and J S Mouton, Gulf Publishing Co, 1965
Corporate Excellence Through Grid Organization Development, R R Blake and J S Mouton, Gulf Publishing Co, 1968

3 Practice of management principles

Coverdale training concentrates on Blake's two primary parameters, the task and the people. The programme aims to promote through experience of group-work on tasks (i) a systematic approach to task performance and (ii) an awareness of the importance and dynamics of building a cohesive and supportive team.

The systematic approach has several stages:

A group must establish its *aim*. 'All practical behaviour is directed in the sense that it is organized around some purpose. This purpose must be explicitly understood and agreed'
A group must organize its available *information* relevant to the aim
The immediate *problem* which requires resolution must be decided. 'Problems are those hurdles which have to be overcome in pursuit of the aim'
The group must *plan* its action; this means asking and answering the questions Who? When? How? Where?
We must *act*; the speed with which we get into action should be related to the risk at stake
Analysis of group performance; this should be based on previously determined success criteria and should concentrate on improving subsequent performance.

Human interaction ('process') learning takes place, as in T-groups, through the intervention of a professional coach and/or an observer appointed by the group from its own membership and through evaluative discussion after a task has been completed. Emphasis is placed on supportive relationships (B's contribution should build on A's) and on improving future performance rather than bemoaning past errors.

The training programme covers three phases, each of one week, during which groups become increasingly independent and autonomous.*

4 Problem analysis and decision making

C H Kepner and B B Tregoe have developed 'a systematic approach to problem solving and decision making', which is based on a training course similar to Coverdale's but with more emphasis on task-oriented decision-making. The essential details of this approach are contained in the diagram (below pp 24–25); it may be necessary to refer to their book for interpretation of terms, but the main areas treated in more detail in the text are the problem analysis and decision making stages.

The Kepner-Tregoe training programme is designed to induce groups of managers to develop this systematic approach to decision making by (i) introducing them to the concepts and methods underlying the approach, (ii) giving them the opportunity to practise on exercises and (iii) feeding back appraisals of their performance.

Participants are provided with study materials which they are expected

**Coverdale Training for Development*, Seamus Roche, Ralph Coverdale, 1967
Thought — A Framework for Teamwork, Ralph Coverdale, Coverdale Training Ltd, 1968

to absorb before the course. When the course convenes, groups are set to work on the problems of a simulated company. The group members have functional positions, can communicate by face-to-face conference or by telephone and are constrained by a strict pressure on time. After the exercise the course leader feeds back a critical evaluation of the use which groups made of their available information.

The one week courses are ideally seen as part of a six-month development programme; on the course individuals receive application study materials and agree with the course leader criteria for measuring improvement in on-the-job performance. Communication takes place between each individual and the course leader at least monthly; and a one or one-and-a-half day review towards the end of the six months is held.

Training programmes have been developed for senior and middle managers (the APEX course); for middle and junior managers (the GENCO course); for sales managers and supervisors (the VERTEX course); and for managers in government agencies and other non-profit organizations (the FBA course). Kepner and Tregoe train and license managers inside companies to run courses and periodically monitor their work to ensure that standards are maintained at a uniformly high level.

Reference

The Rational Manager: A Systematic Approach to Problem Solving and Decision Making, C H Kepner and B B Tregoe, McGraw-Hill, 1965

5 The 3-D organizational effectiveness programme

W J Reddin's management and organizational development training programme is based on his grid model of managerial behaviour. This extends Blake's Grid by adding to 'task orientation' and 'relationships orientation' a third dimension, 'effectiveness'. The eight managerial types derived from this grid are shown in the diagram on page 26.

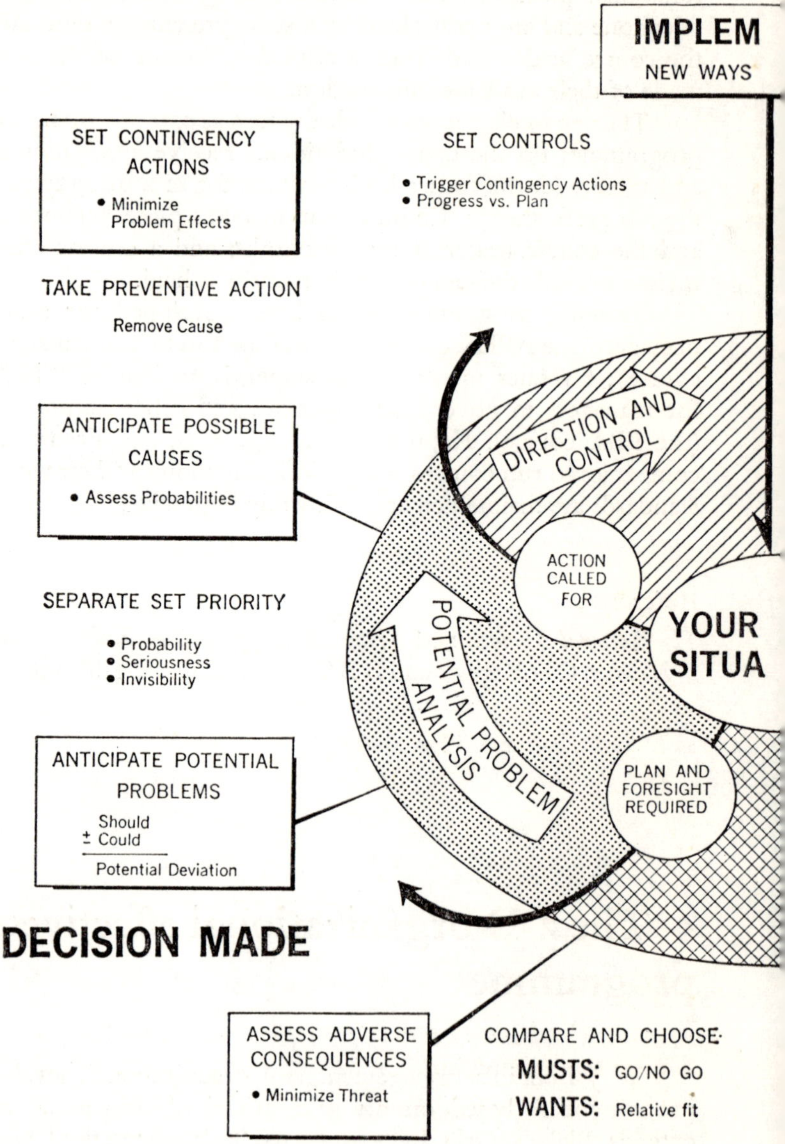
IMPLEM
NEW WAYS
SET CONTINGENCY ACTIONS
• Minimize Problem Effects
SET CONTROLS
• Trigger Contingency Actions
• Progress vs. Plan
TAKE PREVENTIVE ACTION
Remove Cause
ANTICIPATE POSSIBLE CAUSES
• Assess Probabilities
DIRECTION AND CONTROL
ACTION CALLED FOR
SEPARATE SET PRIORITY
• Probability
• Seriousness
• Invisibility
YOUR SITUA
POTENTIAL PROBLEM ANALYSIS
ANTICIPATE POTENTIAL PROBLEMS
Should
± Could
Potential Deviation
PLAN AND FORESIGHT REQUIRED
DECISION MADE
ASSESS ADVERSE CONSEQUENCES
• Minimize Threat
COMPARE AND CHOOSE
MUSTS: GO/NO GO
WANTS: Relative fit

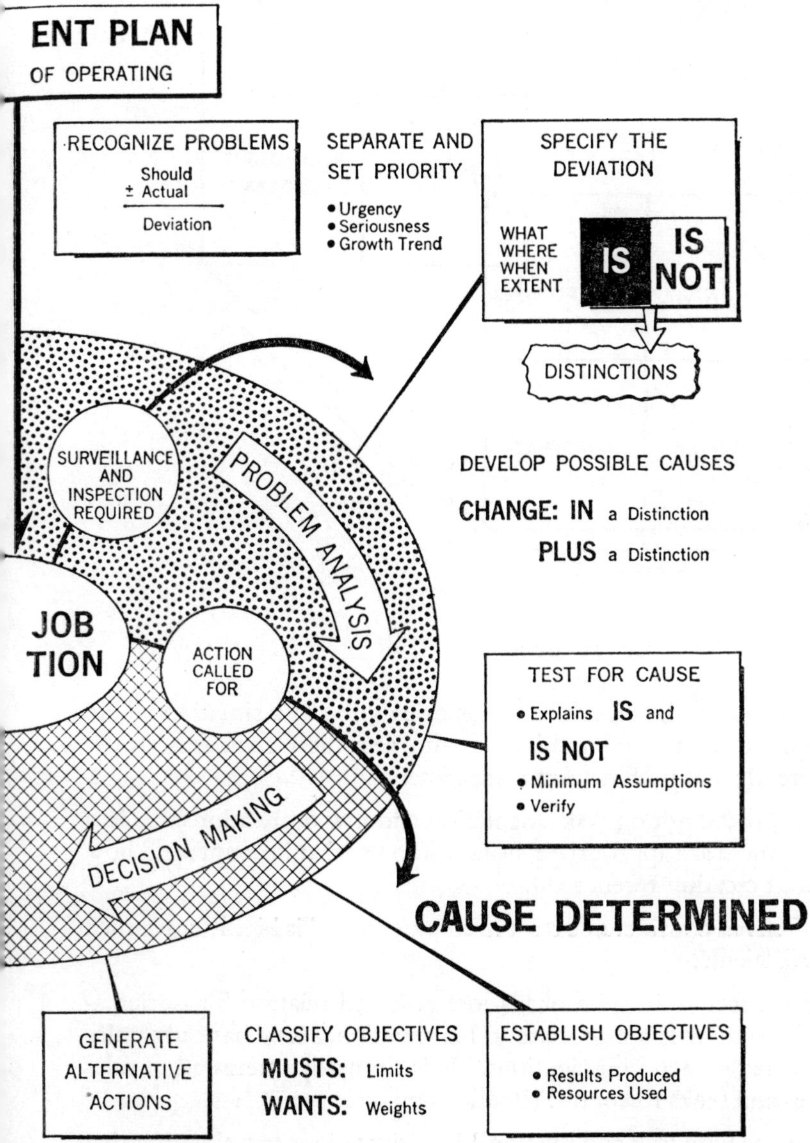
ENT PLAN
OF OPERATING
RECOGNIZE PROBLEMS
Should
± Actual
Deviation
SEPARATE AND
SET PRIORITY
• Urgency
• Seriousness
• Growth Trend
SPECIFY THE
DEVIATION
WHAT
WHERE
WHEN
EXTENT
IS
IS
NOT
DISTINCTIONS
SURVEILLANCE
AND
INSPECTION
REQUIRED
PROBLEM ANALYSIS
DEVELOP POSSIBLE CAUSES
CHANGE: IN a Distinction
PLUS a Distinction
JOB
TION
ACTION
CALLED
FOR
TEST FOR CAUSE
• Explains IS and
IS NOT
• Minimum Assumptions
• Verify
DECISION MAKING
CAUSE DETERMINED
GENERATE
ALTERNATIVE
ACTIONS
CLASSIFY OBJECTIVES
MUSTS: Limits
WANTS: Weights
ESTABLISH OBJECTIVES
• Results Produced
• Resources Used

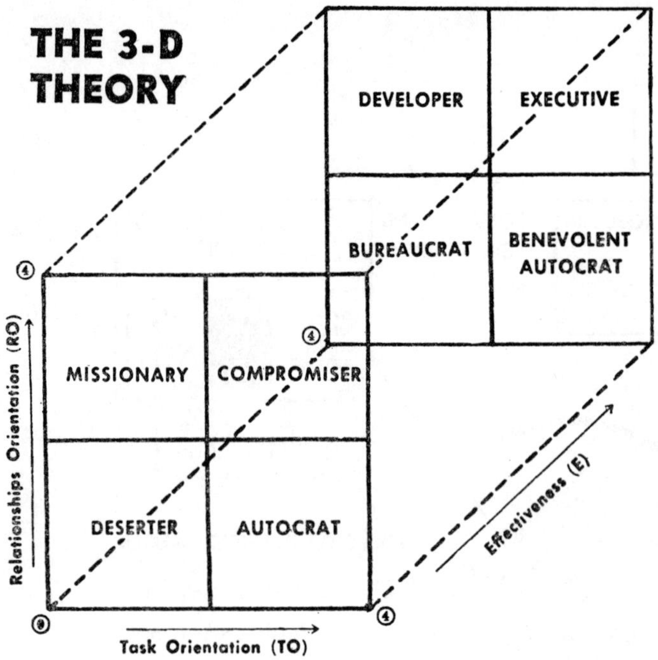

The characteristics of each style are:

The executive, high on task and relationships orientation in a situation where this is appropriate, is a good motivator who sets high standards, treats everyone differently and prefers team management.

The benevolent autocrat, high on task orientation and low on relationships in a situation where these are appropriate, usually knows what he wants and how to get it without creating resentment.

The developer often has considerable trust in employees and is highly concerned to develop their talents.

The bureaucrat is effective in spite of his low task and relationships orientations as such behaviour is appropriate to his situation. He is basically uninvolved but is often seen as conscientious. He is primarily interested in rules and procedures and seeks to control situations by their use.

The compromiser has high task and relationships orientations in a situation that requires high orientation to one or neither to be effective. He is a poor decision maker and allows pressures in the situation to influence him too much. He tends to minimize immediate problems rather than maximize long term production.

The autocrat is often seen as having no confidence in others, unpleasant and only interested in the short term.

The missionary is primarily interested in harmony and is unwilling to risk a disruption of relationships in order to complete a task faster or more effectively.

The deserter tends to be uninvolved and passive.

Reddin provides an easily completed test which enables a manager to identify his own style.

The 3-D Organizational Effectiveness Programme consists of nine stages:

Managerial style seminar-laboratory (five days) This stage is designed to teach 3-D theory, improve a manager's situational diagnostic skill and style flexibility and provide the equipment for assessing the style of oneself and others.

Team role style laboratory (three days)
When preparedness for change and situational and style analysis have been induced by Stage 1, a manager and his subordinates come together in Stage 2 to discuss ways in which they can improve their corporate work. They concentrate on their roles and communication relationships and take part in a team reorganization exercise and team objective setting and decision making exercises.

Managerial objectives conference (four hours)
This stage is designed to strengthen the connection between manager and subordinate. They explore together the job to be done, the factors inhibiting optimum performance, the subordinate's objectives over six months or a year and the support he needs to achieve them.

Corporate strategy laboratory (three days)
This stage involves the senior management group in reviewing the existing long-term objectives of the organization, the flexibility of short-term goals, design effectiveness criteria, policies and managerial philosophy. Through a variety of structured activities and measuring devices, these are held up for inspection and plans made to modify them if necessary.

Team effectiveness conference (one day)
This stage consists of teams reviewing their progress towards agreed objectives and redefining them if necessary.

Team-team effectiveness conference (one day)
Two organizational units describe their own actual and the other's perceived

objectives. The discussion is intended to reduce the discrepancy and lead to more effective interaction in the future.

Divisional effectiveness conference (one day)
This is a multi-level discussion of mutual problems and possibilities for change. This stage is intended to develop strong vertical bonds in the organization.

Work-unit idea conference (four hours)
This discussion is led by foremen and is designed to elicit ideas for job improvement and promote commitment through the acceptance of sound ideas.

Corporate effectiveness conference (four hours)
A large-scale meeting for announcement and discussion of past, present and future policy.

The flexible nature of this training programme is stressed: the stages may be used in different combinations depending on the change objectives. The principles of each stage are designed not only to form the basis of a special programme but also to be built into the organization as an ongoing activity to ensure continued effectiveness.

The main advantages claimed for this programme are:

Effectiveness is emphasized at each stage
It is flexible in operation and may be tailored to meet the needs of individual companies
If desired, all stages may be conducted internally with a minimum of training
The programme does not focus unduly on personality and does not require highly personal feedback
The programme is based on a management style model which is theoretically sound and makes practical sense.

Reference

The 3-D Organizational Effectivess Program, W J Reddin, *Training and Development Journal*, March 1968. *Reproduced by permission.*

6 Training for leadership

Adair's 'training for leadership' is based on a functional approach to a leader's situation: 'Leadership lies in the provisions of the functions necessary for a group to achieve its task and to be held together as a working team.' A leader has to integrate three separate but sometimes overlapping demands: the requirements of the task, the maintenance of the work-team and the meeting of individual needs.

Adair has developed a leadership course which has the following stages:

Explanation of a theory of leadership
Exercises; in the defence services where the approach has been developed these are often field exercises
Feedback on success in achieving and integrating the three primary leadership functions
Discussion relating the exercise lessons to 'back-home' situations
Case study
Final discussion

In addition to the need for such courses, Adair stresses the need for organizations to consider three other factors:

The structure of the organization; does its shape encourage the development of leadership?
The training of training staff; Adair argues that the ideal instructor needs a natural ability and experience as a leader in his own sphere, a working knowledge of the general theory of leadership at a greater depth and width than the level on which he is expected to teach and reasonable skill in a variety of educational methods.
An organization needs research and advisory staff considering both leadership training processes.

Reference

Training for Leadership, J Adair, MacDonald, 1968

7 Achievement-motivation

A training programme to promote 'achievement-motivation' has been based on David McLelland's research into its characteristics. He has established that achievement-motivation is related to the following characteristics:

Ready response to challenge
Greater efforts and demands on self especially in adverse circumstances

Satisfaction in achievement for its own sake
Moderate approach to risk-taking – big enough to offer excitement and hope of worthwhile gain but small enough to ensure that the results were influenced by personal contribution and not by luck
Liking for prompt and precise feedback on progress
Realism about ability and opportunities
Future orientation
Practicality and determination
Preoccupation with and dedication to goals.

McLelland has established through research in many countries that achievement-motivated managers are particularly likely to gain positions of considerable power and responsibility. Although he relates achievement-motivation to early upbringing factors (the most likely breeding grounds for achievement seekers are homes where children are encouraged to begin taking control of their lives at an early age, where they are not excessively restricted by parental discipline and where the emphasis is on preparing them for effectiveness and responsibility as an adult), McLelland has also found that achievement-motivation is subject to considerable advancement among adults.

A course designed to increase participants' awareness and aspiration for 'achievement-motivation' has the following stages:

Initial consideration of the relationship of achievement-motivation to performance and success and discussion of the reasons
Self-testing of achievement-motivation
Evaluation of work approach and setting of realistic challenging goals
Participants practise 'achievement thinking' by learning to perceive job situations in achievement terms. They engage in achievement-related activities in a simulated business situation
Successful entrepreneurs, either in person or through case material, are presented to participants to enable them to see the relationship between successful business functioning and achievement thinking and to understand the origins of entrepreneural behaviour
Lectures, discussions and demonstrations involving creative problem-solving and risk-taking in order that participants experience and internalize the characteristics of a successful entrepreneur
Participants are encouraged to write an autobiography, make plans for their future, take the practical steps and make the commitments necessary to fulfil their goals. Personal counselling sessions are arranged for individuals to obtain better self-knowledge, more realistic appraisal of goals and more creative ways of attaining them

Participants are helped to understand the needs of other group members and to help them resolve their problems
Participants practise mutual support in group activities to increase their post-course cooperation
Contact is maintained between course members and tutors for two years during which participants write regular progress reports which are analysed and criticized by staff. If their situation is conducive, participants are encouraged to form an association designed to stimulate economic growth for the purpose of maintaining the achievement spirit.

Reference

Motivating Economic Achievement, D C McLelland *et al*, Collier-MacMillan, © 1969. *Reproduced by permission.*

8 The technology of training

Some behavioural scientists adopt a systems approach to the training process and have developed the following model (see page 32).

The analysis of the overall system involves determining its needs and the most appropriate way in which these can best be met. In some cases work simplification, job reorganization, the provision of job-aids, improved equipment design etc may be more appropriate than a training programme.
Job analysis defines the particular tasks constituting an overall job and establishes their frequency, importance, difficulty etc. The end product is a job description, ie a listing of the activities of the experienced worker.
Measures of proficiency must be available in the design of training programmes.
Job specification is mainly concerned with the knowledge and skills required for successful performance on the job.
The knowledge and skills already possessed by trainees must also be measured. It is the difference between the attainments, aptitudes and attitudes possessed by the trainee and those needed for success in the job which defines the training requirements.
The selection of appropriate methods is the central problem. The five principles which seem important are:

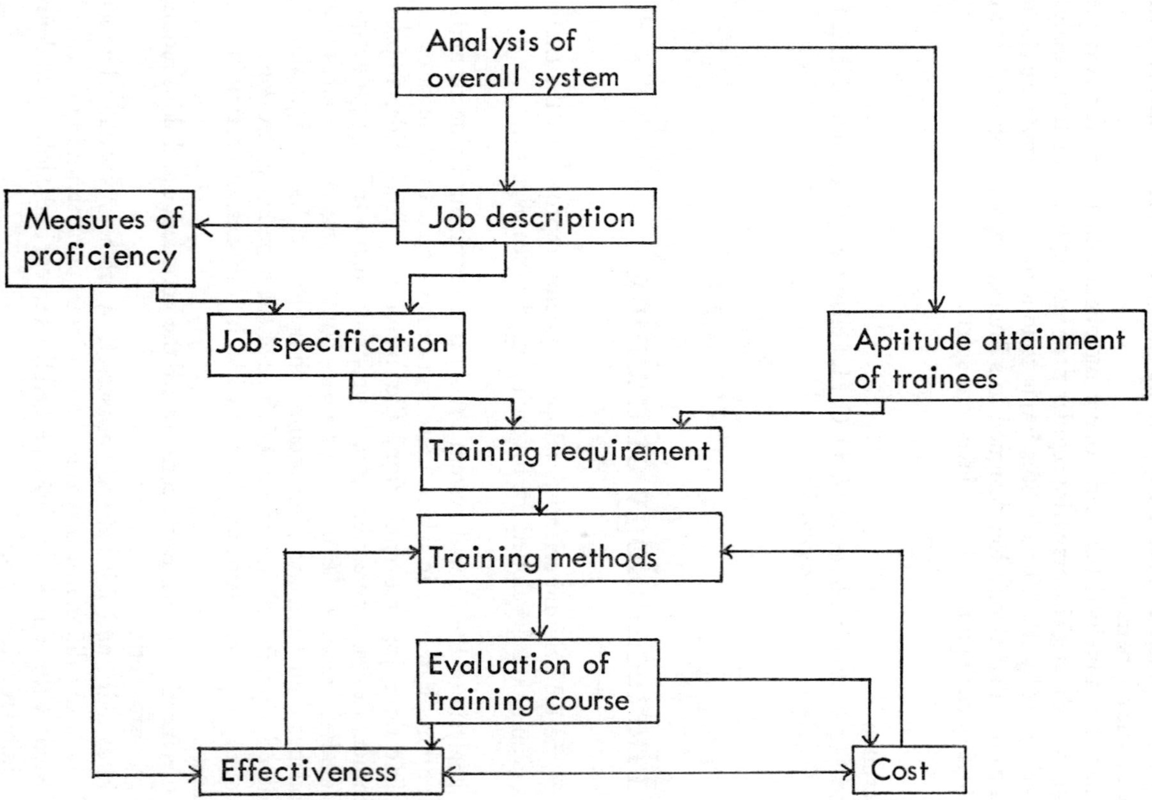
Analysis of overall system
Job description
Measures of proficiency
Job specification
Aptitude attainment of trainees
Training requirement
Training methods
Evaluation of training course
Effectiveness
Cost

(a) the material to be learned must appear meaningful to the learner; if it does it will be more easily absorbed and retained
(b) the opportunity to practise must be provided; the material which is overlearned is better retained and more resistant to loss in times of stress
(c) feedback about progress being made must be available to the trainee. 'Practice makes perfect' is not true. Knowledge about *progress* is also essential
(d) Transfer from the training to the real-life situation must be optimized
(e) Evaluation of the course in cost-effectiveness terms is crucial. If trainees fail to pass the criterion test it may be the fault of the course. Even where the methods have proved effective, there might still be room for an improvement in the utilization of resources.

Reference

Industrial Society, (Chapter 5), D Pym, Penguin, 1968

CHANGE-FACILITATION TECHNIQUES

1 Job enrichment

Job enrichment is a motivational tool developed by Frederick Herzberg on the basis of extensive study of factors affecting job satisfaction. His research conclusions were that satisfaction and dissatisfaction in work are not based on positive and negative manifestations of the same factors but on completely different factors. Characteristics of the job *content* (ie achievement, recognition, interest of the work, responsibility, advancement, growth) are likely to induce extreme satisfaction in work; shortcomings in the job *context* (ie company policy and administration, supervision, relationship with supervisor, working conditions, salary, relationship with peers, personal life, relationship with subordinates, status and security) are likely to lead to extreme dissatisfaction in work.

Job enrichment is concerned to design work so that the influence of motivating factors can be maximized. Herzberg is careful to distinguish job enrichment from job enlargement; job enlargement tends to increase the *amount* of work through higher target-setting, job rotation etc; job enrichment seeks to provide the opportunity for psychological growth through changing the nature of the work.

The seven main principles of job enrichment are:

'Removing some controls while retaining accountability
Increasing the accountability of individuals for own work
Giving a person a complete natural unit of work
Granting additional authority to an employee in his activity; job freedom

Making periodic reports directly available to the worker himself rather than to the supervisor
Introducing new and more difficult tasks not previously handled
Assigning individuals specific or specialized tasks, enabling them to become experts.'

Herzberg recommends that the introduction of job enrichment to a group of workers should be monitored by a controlled experiment. At least two equivalent groups should be chosen, one an experimental unit in which the motivators are systematically introduced over a period, the other a control group in which no changes are made. For both groups the job *context* (what Herzberg calls its 'hygiene') should be allowed to follow its natural course for the duration of the experiment. Pre- and post-installation tests of performance and job attitudes are necessary to evaluate the effectiveness of the job enrichment programme.

References

The Motivation to Work, Herzberg, Mansner and Snyderman, Wiley, 1959
One More Time: How do you Motivate Employees? F. Herzberg, *Harvard Business Review*. Jan/Feb, 1968

2 Planned change

Planned change is described by Warren Bennis as a 'method which encompasses the application of systematic and appropriate knowledge to human affairs for the purpose of creating intelligent action and choices.'

Change takes place through a 'collaborative relationship' between a 'change-agent', typically an external behavioural scientist contracted to give advice and the 'client-system', the organization which is the target of change. They seek to apply 'valid knowledge' derived from behavioural science research to the client-systems's problems and change-requirements.

The 'deliberate and collaborative relationship' between the change-agent and the client-system requires five distinguishing features to ensure optimal planned change:

The change programme is undertaken jointly; goals are mutually determined
A 'spirit of enquiry' pervades the relationship; the relationship is 'governed by data, publicly shared'

The relationship grows out of 'mutual interaction of the client and the change-agent'
The relationship is voluntary with either free to bring about its termination after joint consultation
'Each party has equal opportunities to influence the other'

The 'normative goals' which change-agents are likely to introduce for discussion with the client are:

"An improvement in the interpersonal competence of managers
A change in values so that human factors and feelings come to be considered legitimate
Development of increased understanding between and within working groups
Development of . . . more effective team management
Development of more rational and open methods of conflict resolution
Development of organic systems, ie organization structures which promote:

relationships between and within groups
mutual confidence and trust
interdependencies and shared responsibility
multigroup membership and responsibility
wide sharing of control and responsibility
conflict resolution through bargaining or problem solving."

References

The Planning of Change, W Benis *et al*, Holt, Rinehart and Winston, 1966
Changing Organizations, W Benis, McGraw-Hill, 1966

3 Participative management

The belief that by making employees happier they would also be more productive arose from the 'human relations school' of behavioural science which originated in the Hawthorne studies. Rensis Likert has refined this approach and bases a 'theory of management systems' on the results of extensive research into the performance characteristics of different types of organization. He delineates four 'management systems': exploitive authoritative (system 1); benevolent authoritative (system 2); consultative (system 3); participative (system 4), and describes them in terms of the following operating characteristics: (*continued p* 38)

If a manager has:
A well-organized plan of operation
High performance goals
High technical competence
(manager or staff assistants)

Causal variables

and if the manager manages via

SYSTEMS 1 or 2	SYSTEM 4
eg uses direct hierarchical pressure for results, including the usual contests and other practices of the traditional systems	eg uses principle of supportive relationships, group methods of supervision, and other principles of System 4

his organization will display

Intervening variables

SYSTEMS 1 or 2	SYSTEM 4
Less group loyalty	Greater group loyalty
Lower performance goals	Higher performance goals
Greater conflict and less cooperation	Greater cooperation
Less technical assistance to peers	More technical assistance to peers
Greater feeling of unreasonable pressure	Less feeling of unreasonable pressure
Less favourable attitudes toward manager	More favourable attitudes toward manager
Lower motivation to produce	Higher motivation to produce

and his organization will attain

End-result variables

SYSTEMS 1 or 2	SYSTEM 4
Lower sales volume	Higher sales volume
Higher sales costs	Lower sales costs
Lower quality of business sold	Higher quality of business sold
Lower earnings by salesmen	Higher earnings by salesmen

motivational forces
communication processes
interaction-influence process
decision-making process
goal-setting or ordering
control processes
performance characteristics

His broad conclusions are summarized in the diagram on page 37.

Likert has established that this model is valid not only in stable conditions but also in times of change. The more an organization's behavioural characteristics approximate system 4, the more productivity, labour relations, costs, earnings etc show long-term improvement.

A similar approach which has had considerable theoretical and practical influence is Douglas McGregor's dichotomization of managers' role-perceptions into Theory X and Theory Y.

The different role-perceptions of Theory X and Theory Y managers are:

"*Theory X*

Management is responsible for organizing the elements of productive enterprise – money, materials, equipment, people – in the interest of economic ends

With respect to people, this is a process of directing their efforts, motivating them, controlling their actions, modifying their behaviour to fit the needs of the organization

Without this active intervention by management, people would be passive – even resistant – to organizational needs. They must therefore be persuaded, rewarded, punished, controlled: their activities must be directed. This is management's task, in managing subordinate managers or workers. We often sum it up by saying that management consists of getting things done through other people.

Theory Y

Management is responsible for organizing the elements of productive enterprise – money, materials, equipment, people – in the interest of economic ends

People are not by nature passive or resistant to organizational needs. They have become so as a result of experience in organizations

The motivation, the potential for development, the capacity for assuming responsibility, the readiness to direct behaviour toward organizational goals are all present in people. Management does not put them there. It is a responsibility of management to make it possible for people to recognize and develop the human characteristics for themselves
The essential task of management is to arrange organizational conditions and methods of operation so that people can achieve their own goals best by directing their own efforts toward organizational objectives."

McGregor has broadly concluded that organizations whose managers are concerned to integrate individual and organizational goals in the Theory Y approach are likely to prove particularly adaptable to changing demands and ensure both employee satisfaction and successful company performance.

References

The Human Organization (Chapters 3 and 4), R Likert, McGraw-Hill, 1967
The Human Side of Enterprise, D McGregor, McGraw-Hill, 1960
Leadership and Motivation, D McGregor, © MIT Press, 1966. *Reproduced by permission.*

4 Management by objectives

Management by objectives is based on the assumption that managers will be more effective and will become committed to objectives if they are involved in establishing them and if they work in an organization which encourages self-control and self-development.

Management by objectives has six main aspects:

Continuous review of the organization's strategy, profit plans etc
The identification, by each manager with his immediate superior, of key task areas of work and the establishment of performance standards and control data
The integration and dovetailing of these performance standards with those of other managers and with unit and organization objectives
The establishment, by each manager and his immediate superior, of job improvement plans outlining short-term targets which will make a contribution to the achievement of performance standards
Regular and systematic performance reviews where progress towards the achievement of short-term targets and longer-term performance standards may be assessed and discussed
Guidance and training to help managers' development.

This process is viewed as dynamic. The company objectives of growth rate, return on investment, market penetration etc are likely to affect the performance standards which are established for individual managers and vice versa. There needs to be a continuous interaction and reconciliation of organization objectives and individual performance standards.

Management by objectives provides techniques and a systematic approach to undergird what management should always have been doing. Its most novel and important feature is emphasis on *joint* establishment of objectives between a manager and his superior. To the extent that 'management by objectives' describes the manager's job, it should be seen as 'a system of managing, not an addition to the manager's job'.

Reference

Improving Business Results, J Humble, McGraw-Hill, 1967

5 Action research

Action research is based on a relationship between a client organization and research institution in which the client undertakes to introduce organzational changes recommended by the researchers and allow these to be monitored.

The behavioural scientist conducts an initial analysis of organizational problems and bases his 'action' recommendations on relevant cumulated theory in his discipline. The changes introduced are the result of discussion between the researcher and the client and need not be strictly in accordance with the researcher's initial recommendations.

The researcher returns to the organization at regular intervals after the introduction of change and measures corresponding alterations in performance, employee attitudes, communication effectiveness and other dependent variables in which he is interested.

Action research is less concerned with the quality of relationship between client and researcher than other change programmes and has considerable advantages both for the researcher and the firm. The researcher is provided with a 'laboratory' in which he can recommend changes and measure their effect; the firm receives the benefit of independent specialist appraisal and advice. Action research differs from consultancy in the absence of a financial agreement and the right retained by the researcher to publish findings. It is also a more deliberately analytical, experimental and long-term approach than is customarily provided for in a consultancy contract.

References

Action Research in a Small Firm, P J Sadler and B A Barry, *Journal of Management Studies*, October 1968

Organizational Development, P J Sadler and B A Barry, Longmans Green, 1970

6 Organization development learning

Organizational development technology sets out to provide a comprehensive framework for the application of the behavioural sciences to organizational practice. Its stages are:

Felt need: the organization perceived the need for change through a specific problem, comparison with other organizations, inability to meet external demands, exposure to new managerial bandwagons etc.

Data collection about the felt need. Internal or external resources may be responsible; it is crucial to determine the *real* need, which may or may not be the need which is felt, and to distinguish between symptom and cause. Data about the overall system, especially forces promoting and inhibiting change, and the resources available to maximize change opportunity are critical.

Data feedback and discussion. If behavioural science specialists have been involved in data collection, discussion and mutual comprehension for its interpretation and significance must occur with management. The diagnosis of organizational ills should never be unilateral.

Realistic objectives should be established for a change programme.

The strategy for change must be determined. This includes consideration of:

- desired outcome
- dependent variable – *what* needs to be changed
- interacting variables – other parts of the system with which the dependent variable interacts and the nature of this interaction
- system boundary for the change; this must be assessed in relation to the intended change effects and available resources
- independent variable; the change tool may be a training programme, job or organization re-design, work planning, technical change etc
- entry point; task, structure, technology and human resources can be seen in a state of continual mutual interaction; it is not always beneficial to enter this system by directly altering the variable which is the ultimate target of change
- timescale, pace, costs etc

Plan the who, what, where, when, how of implementing the strategy

Action

Review

Conclusion

The 22 techniques of behavioural science application outlined in this publication have been presented neutrally. Although the juxtaposition and brief exposition of each technique should aid comparison, it is hoped that any evaluative conclusions drawn by readers will be limited and tentative. Not only is this booklet the first rather than the last word on the techniques: judgements *in vacuo* are inappropriate. Each technique can only be seen as good, bad or irrelevant in relation to particular organizational circumstances and needs. Each reader will need to ask, 'What is there in these techniques, not in general terms, but for me and my organization?'

The techniques are situation-specific in their utility. But I should like to conclude by suggesting four general considerations likely to apply in any attempt to use them:

(i) the relationship between analysis, training and change-facilitation
(ii) an overall perspective on behavioural science techniques
(iii) relationship dynamics between client organizations and behavioural science technicians
(iv) the implications which use of behavioural science techniques have for intra-organizational relationships.

Each of these areas is huge and complex and intimation of lines of thought is all that is possible. It nevertheless seems important to introduce some of the *non*-technical issues likely to arise in the consideration of behavioural science techniques.

The relationship between analysis, training and change-facilitation

Any of the techniques can be used in an organization, separately or in conjunction, at any time. However, the most accurate answer to the question posed above – 'so what for my organization?' – will be reached on the basis of analysis. Only full analysis of an organization's circumstances will suggest the training or change-facilitation technique(s) most likely to meet its needs. It is only through analysis that an organization can determine what it is changing *from* – a vital factor in any discussion about what to change *to*. Only analysis makes subsequent change *evaluation* possible; without it the baseline is lost for ever. Use of behavioural science techniques therefore optimally starts with analysis (though it has to be emphasized that this particular piece of 'sense' has not proved all that 'common' in the past!). On the basis of determined need, decisions can be made about the training and/or change-facilitation programme(s) required. On the whole, the more an overall change programme can be settled on, with training components being fitted in as and when appropriate, the more effective will both the change-facilitation and the training be.

An overall perspective on behavioural science techniques

Much enthusiasm has been generated by behavioural science techniques; but they have also caused heart- (and head-!) aches. The latter might have been avoided if the techniques had been seen in their proper perspective. They are basically tools; their actual and potential power is exciting; but their real-life limitations spell caution. They contain no magic. They offer no panaceas (and if their marketing material does, it should be discounted). They are based on limited and often inconclusive behavioural science evidence (this is better than none but its conditional nature should be recognized). They cannot *guarantee* any effects, still less that these will be favourable.

The techniques contain and offer enough to suggest that their use could, and probably should, benefit organizations. Their payoffs are likely to be higher (and meet managerial expectations more readily), the more they are used to promote changes which are short-term, small-scale and, most importantly, seen as experimental. This is not to devalue the techniques; technical developments in the natural sciences have generally advanced one step at a time; so, too, will personnel and organizational developments based on the behavioural sciences.

Relationship dynamics between client organizations and behavioural science technicians

The more analysis is conducted by an organization, the more are its real needs clarified; and the more they are likely to be exposed as interrelated and complex. The tools of behavioural change appropriate to meet such needs will usually be multi-disciplinary and flexible. But this requirement frequently conflicts with the nature of the techniques on offer. At their worst, behavioural science techniques can be seen as superficial and one-dimensional. Even at best, there has been a tendency for behavioural science technicians to adopt an all-or-nothing approach to marketing; prospective client organizations have been expected to take (or leave) total packages (their wrapping paper often containing misleading answer-to-all-ills claims). The risk has been run, and frequently lost, by the technicians, of rejection by potential consumers; in the process the behavioural-science-technique baby is thrown out with its marketing bath water.

Behavioural science technicians are becoming more reality-based; but user organizations should exert constant pressure on them to meet the real needs of a concrete situation. Organizations should conduct business with behavioural science technicians as with any other contractors. They should decide what they want from them and ensure, for the duration of a project, that all goods are both delivered and as tailor-made as is required. This is the only way of bridging the divide in kind between demand and supply.

In concentrating on factors in client-technician relationships, it should not be forgotten that a real-life alternative is some form of do-it-yourself. DIY is an implicit principle of many of the techniques and should offer considerable achievement-motivation challenge to personnel, and other, managers! As long as an organization's technical limitations are recognized (and, if necessary, compensated for with a little help from its behavioural science friends), do-it-yourself (or, at least, the full participation of the organization's own staff in the running of a programme) may well be the most effective (as well as attractive) approach to using behavioural science techniques.

The implications of using behavioural science techniques for intra-organizational relationships

The simplistic use of the term 'client organization' in preceding sections disguises the reality that many different work groups/departments are likely to have a stake in deciding about, or using, behavioural science techniques. Unless representatives of all interested parties are involved in making decisions about, or reviewing the progress of, a programme which employs behavioural science techniques, there is a danger that the favourable results expected by those who do decide might be sabotaged by those who do not. This applies both to inter-department relationships and to management/staff/worker relations, whether or not channelled through formal industrial relations procedures. Trade unions in particular have been cool towards the use of behavioural science techniques. This is partly because their interests have not been met; partly because they have not been seen to be met (eg through involvement in effective decision-making processes); and partly because the techniques are seen as potentially expoitative: hardly surprisingly when (i) management retains the whip-hand in decision-making and (ii) further increases its power by using the techniques to obtain (and use, often to its own advantage) otherwise unavailable information from employees.

Power-sharing must characterize the use of behavioural science techniques. Departments initiating a project should ensure that others likely to be affected have the opportunity to take part in policy and practice supervisory committees. Such committees should also comprise representatives of trade unions and employee work groups.

Power-sharing in the use of behavioural science techniques will promote more widely accepted and therefore more thorough-going change. It will also, incidentally but importantly, provide a safeguard (possibly the only, certainly the most powerful) against the *ab*-use of behavioural science techniques by sectional interests.

The techniques could form effective instruments in the attainment of whatever destiny collective man chooses for industrial society. Their abuse could promote 1984. These ethical cum political, as well as technical, issues should be recognized, and reconciled, in any decision to use the techniques of application being developed through behavioural science.

IPM Publications

Our current catalogue includes publications of immediate interest to line managers as well as to professional personnel and training managers and students. It now contains over 70 titles.

Members may purchase publications at preferential rates, and generous discounts are available on bulk orders.

If you would like a free copy of our catalogue please write to: Publication Sales Dept, Institute of Personnel Management, 5 Winsley Street, Oxford Circus, London WIN 7AQ.

Some of our recent publications are described here.

Industrial Tribunals
Roger Greenhalgh
This book aims to provide a guide for the individual, whether employee or employer, for whom the likelihood of an appearance before an Industrial Tribunal has increased in the light of recent legislation. Roger Greenhalgh describes the history and philosophy of Industrial Tribunals, their procedures from the Originating Application to the judgement – and after, and details the preparation and presentation of a case.
£2·00; £1·50 IPM members 224 pp 0 85292 084 9

Collective Bargaining in Western Europe
Information Report 13
Examines the arrangements for collective bargaining in the countries of Western Europe, concentrating on the enlarged European Community. The report covers the legal framework, the parties to collective agreements, the levels at which bargaining takes place and the content of agreements. It looks at what happens in dispute cases and points to developments and future trends.
£2·00; £1·25 IPM members 0 85292 081 4

Developing Resourceful Managers

John Morris and John G Burgoyne

Management development is often seen as an important but rather predictable activity: the skilled task of making sure that the enterprize is effectively managed both in the present and foreseeable future.

Developing managers then becomes an affair for personnel specialists – a set of elaborate and sophisticated techniques rather than an exchange of ideas and the expression of strong feeling.

While the authors are aware of the need for planning and control, they also want to bring out the need for able managers to develop themselves.

£1; 75p IPM members 85 pp 0 85292 078 4

Coming to Terms with Trade Unions

W E J McCarthy and A S Collier

This book is about the nature of the challenge which trade unionism presents to management and the steps which management has to take to deal with it.

Six case studies show how ways of dealing with employees are found to be increasingly inappropriate as unions gain recognition and extend collective bargaining in a given firm or industry. The emphasis throughout is on strategy rather than tactics, on the questions that need to be answered if trade union–management relations are to be improved and adapted to fit changing circumstances over the medium and long term.

£1·25; 80p IPM members 163 pp 0 85292 077 6

Management Training for Real

Hawdon Hague

Little attention has been paid until recently to setting management training in a real context and the idea of trainers without classrooms and syndicate rooms seems almost bizarre.

In this new approach the trainer makes learning capital out of whatever turns up, or so structures the actual situation that maximum learning takes place. In either case it is *the situation* that provides the opportunity and the stimulus for the manager to develop himself – which is the key to the learning impact.

Hawdon Hague shows that assumptions and preconceptions about management training have to be changed. He spells out what to do and why, what reorientation is necessary and the dangers to avoid.

£1·25; 80p IPM members 128 pp 085292 083 0

Flexible Working Hours
Information Report 12
J M Hill
UK companies which have introduced flexible working hours have found support from an overwhelming majority of employees. Most employees tend to modify their working hours only slightly, yet a return to conventional working hours according to one personnel officer would 'cause a riot'. IPM's new information report considers flexible working in the UK, West Germany France and Switzerland and finishes with a selected reading list and a list of manufacturers of variable time recording equipment.
£1·50; 80p IPM members 0 85292 074 1

Human Asset Accounting
W J Giles and D F Robinson
A joint working party was set up in the autumn of 1970 by the IPM and the Institute of Cost and Management Accountants to attempt to solve the problem of measuring the value of the human factor in business and commerce. The tool to be fashioned from the concept of human asset accounting, which the authors describe here, could help to increase understanding of the importance of people in an organization's affairs with consequent economic and social advantages.
£1·25; 75p IPM members 30 pp 0 85292 075 x

Staff Appraisal
G A Randell, P M A Packard, R L Shaw and A J Slater
Cuts through the myths and assertions surrounding the purposes and techniques of staff appraisal and sets out a practical approach to the subject. The basic principles of staff appraisal are given in Part I and these principles are described in practice in Part II.
70p; 55p IPM members 79 pp 0 85292 073 3

Perspectives in Manpower Planning
The Edinburgh Group
Everyone talks about the importance of manpower planning and yet few agree on what it is and how it can be practised. This pamphlet is intended in part to provide a practical guide on manpower planning for those who work in organizations—companies, universities, hospitals or banks.
60p 93 pp 0 85292 060 1